The Phoenix Living Poets

SURROUNDINGS

The Phoenix Living Poets

MEASURES
Norman MacCaig
THIS COLD UNIVERSE
THE WORLD I SEE
Patric Dickinson
ADDICTIONS
THE OLD ADAM
D. J. Enright
WHEN THAT APRIL
Gillian Stoneham
POEMS
Lotte Zurndorfer
SELECTED POEMS
NIGHTS AND DAYS
James Merrill
THE SUN MY MONUMENT
Laurie Lee
FAIRGROUND MUSIC
John Fuller
NATURE WITH MAN
Jon Silkin
CONTROL TOWER
Richard Kell
THE SWANS OF BERWICK
Sydney Tremayne
POEMS
Alexander Baird
THE YEAR OF THE WHALE
George Mackay Brown
THE DIRECTIONS OF MEMORY
Laurence Lerner
SELECTED POEMS
Robert Pack
THE BURNING HARE
J. C. Hall
MEN WITHOUT EVENINGS
David Gill
FINDING GOLD
Leslie Norris
ON THE WAY TO THE DEPOT
P. J. Kavanagh

SURROUNDINGS

by

NORMAN MacCAIG

CHATTO AND WINDUS

THE HOGARTH PRESS

1967

Published by
Chatto and Windus Ltd
42 William IV Street
London WC2

*

Clarke, Irwin and Co Ltd
Toronto

First Published 1966
Reprinted 1967

Printed in Great Britain by
T. H. Brickell and Son Ltd
The Blackmore Press, Gillingham, Dorset

Contents

Contents

Metaphysical Me

He fawned on objects.
He serenaded the dust in the streets
And made himself ridiculous about fish.
There wasn't an interruption of space
He didn't flatter, saying
It was an interruption of time.
Politicians
Didn't understand him.

Naturally this bred ideas
About the nature of being
And habits,
Which are the nature of being;
So that, when, after thirty years
As an infinite bigamist,
He grew bored and wanted to divorce the lot,
He found he couldn't
For the sake of the children.

Humanism

When the glacier was defeated
In the siege of Suilven and limped off
To the East, it left behind it all that
Burdened its retreat –
Stones, the size of
Sandgrains and haystacks:
Abandoned loot of Glen Canisp.

What a human lie is this. What greed and what
Arrogance, not to allow
A glacier to be a glacier –
To humanise into a metaphor
That long slither of ice – that was no more
A beaten army than it was a horde
Of Cinderellas, each,
When her midnight sounded,
Leaving behind her
A sandstone shoe.

I defend the glacier that
When it absorbs a man
Preserves his image
Intact.

Go-Between

Out of a night
That felt like a grape's skin
An owl's voice shuddered.
Out of the running
Blackness of a river pool
A white salmon unplugged
Itself and fell back
In a smash of light.
Out of the throat of
A duck flying over,
Delicate, Japanese
On the blue plate of the sky,
Came a croaking grunt,
Catarrhal and fat-living.
Out of your never
Averted face, come
Classical admonitions
Of the finality of form
And the untrespassable regions
Beyond it. I go
Poaching there and come
Back with news of
An owl's hoot, exploding
Salmon and the profound eructations
From the flat nose of
A delicate duck.

Since I am your convert
And true believer, I have
To enlarge the admonitions
Of your never averted face
To include these wild regions

Where the lunacy of form
Is normal and caricature
Impossible. Am I bringing
Your news to them or their news
To you? Am I evangelising
The duck or you? – For how can a man
Breathe hymns to the Lord
With one lung and hymns to the devil
With the other?

Cloud of Undoing

I sit
Dissolving myself
Into an environment
Without me.

A water splash
On a granite stone
Vanishes so gradually and
So all at once
It leaves behind it
No smile in the air.

An unravelled man
Is spreading away
Into disappearances.

The puff of mist on
A rib of Stac Polly
After being a veil
And a stain
Is a rib of Stac Polly.

I move
Into vanished things,
Taking their vanishing
With me.

After the veil, the stain,
After the stain, the rib,
After the rib
Stac Polly.

The Streets of Florence

Tired of these ordinary heads carrying
From somewhere else to somewhere or other
Their ordinary ambitions and lusts and boredoms,
I turned aside into the Uffizi Gallery
And submerged myself in the throng
Of undying presences, created once
In the minds of great painters and
Continuously creating themselves ever since.

When I went out again
Into the steep sunlight, I saw with astonishment
These undying presences had climbed down
From the walls and with an unconvincing
Change of clothes were carrying
Their extraordinary heads from one
Great rendezvous to another.

I, then? What am I
A continuing creation of? What Hebridean
Island and what century have I failed
To escape from in the dangerous journey
From my first great rendezvous to the one
I have still to keep?

Progress

When the armies marched off,
Cursing the criminal stupidity of their leaders,
To fight for the glory and prosperity
Of the motherland,
The leaders
Did their bit
By putting the prices up;
And when the remnants came back,
Cursing the criminal stupidity of their leaders,
Their leaders did what they could for them
By putting the prices up again.
This so reduced
The prosperity of the country
That new leaders were appointed
Whose criminal stupidity was no less
Than the first.

The only consoling thought is
That somewhere along the line
The idea of glory
Was lost sight of.

Three Invisibles

The sea is invisible
Under a sun-scatter of light.

What are you invisible under?
From what hard foreland of being
Do I fail to see you?

I could put a boat
Into that baffling glitter
That would tame it, that would slide
On the veriest water . . .

Inland, the mountains
Withdraw
Behind a beautiful blue haze.

Is your beauty a thing
That comes between me and you?
Is what strips me
To my unwilling self
Your closest shelter?

I could walk through that haze
And reach those mountains,
I could measure them
With legs and lungs.

What wrong place am I in
Who, of three invisible things,
Love most the one
No voyage will take me to,
No journey will ever take me to?

Frogs

Frogs sit more solid
Than anything sits. In mid-leap they are
Parachutists falling
In a free fall. They die on roads
With arms across their chests and
Heads high.

I love frogs that sit
Like Buddha, that fall without
Parachutes, that die
Like Italian tenors.

Above all, I love them because,
Pursued in water, they never
Panic so much that they fail
To make stylish triangles
With their ballet dancer's
Legs.

King of Beasts

To come close to a city
Is a hard matter
For one man – all these hawks
And crocodiles, milch-cows and
Pretty posies, sting-nettles and basking
Sharks wear human faces. Easy
For a man-fox to recognise
A man-fox or a blue hare being
A man; but how is he to know
A disguised shrimp or a nightingale
With a pipe in its mouth?

– The only one
There's no mistake about is
The indifferent lion lolling
Through the jungle in the back of
His Rolls-Royce. When you see him,
Keep off the Zebra crossing – dive
Down an alley, if you're a rabbit,
Or sing, if you're a lark,
Straight up in the air.

Interruption to a Journey

The hare we had run over
Bounced about the road
On the springing curve
Of its spine.

Cornfields breathed in the darkness.
We were going through the darkness and
The breathing cornfields from one
Important place to another.

We broke the hare's neck
And made that place, for a moment,
The most important place there was,
Where a bowstring was cut
And a bow broken for ever
That had shot itself through so many
Darknesses and cornfields.

It was left in that landscape.
It left us in another.

Porpoises

In twos and threes and fives
They made a circus-ring of the Minch,
Wheeling over, and leaving behind them in the air
Two puffs, three puffs, five puffs –
Audible plumes.
One looked to see on their backs
Or in the carved car they might well be pulling
Some plump mythical boy
Or sea-green sea-nymph
Or Arion himself, twangling from his lyre
Audible spray.

But not
These days.

All the same, I myself
(In a mythical sort of way)
Have been drawn over metaphorical waters
By these curving backs, till,
Filled with an elation
I don't want to have explained to me,
I lifted a pagan face and shouted
Audible nonsense.

Sounds of the Day

When a clatter came,
It was horses crossing the ford.
When the air creaked, it was
A lapwing seeing us off the premises
Of its private marsh. A snuffling puff
Ten yards from the boat was the tide blocking,
Unblocking a hole in a rock.
When the black drums rolled, it was water
Falling sixty feet into itself.

When the door
Scraped shut, it was the end
Of all the sounds there are.

You left me
Beside the quietest fire in the world.

I thought I was hurt in my pride only,
Forgetting that,
When you plunge your hand in freezing water,
You feel
A bangle of ice round your wrist
Before the whole hand goes numb.

Two-Part Invention

With evidences to choose from
I am bludgeoned by the ones
I do not choose.

With reasons for loving you
I am continually being trapped
By what are no reasons for loving you at all.

Both these things
Reveal a certain foolish helplessness –
But there's a man inside me
Cleverer than I,
The hidden persuaded,
Who hears sounds beyond my reach,
Is not to be deceived by disguises
And is familiar with the invisible.
This makes me, not him,
Vulnerable.

Sometimes he speaks for me with my voice, saying
Things like –
"With plenty of time to think of you,
I think of you only
When I am busiest – that is,
When I am thinking of you."

Smuggler

Watch him when he opens
His bulging words – justice,
Fraternity, freedom, internationalism, peace,
Peace, peace. Make it your custom
To pay no heed
To his frank look, his visas, his stamps
And signatures. Make it
Your duty to spread out their contents
In a clear light.

Nobody with such luggage
Has nothing to declare.

Responsibility

They left the horse standing for two days
With a shattered leg
Till the vet signed a paper.
Then they dug a hole beside it
And put a bullet in its skull.
They didn't consider its wishes
When they did either of those things.

This could have been worse only
If they had had to wait
Till the horse signed a paper.

Some day they'll dig a hole
Near enough to the vet's bed
For him to know it's there.
Let him write that off,
Let him sign himself out of that
When he's lying there with a face on him
As white as bone.

Waiting to Notice

I sprawl among seapinks – a statue
Fallen from the ruins
Of the air into
The twentieth century – and think:
A crowd of fancies is not so easily come by
As you suppose. They have to happen
Like weather, or a migration, or a haystack
Going up in flames all on its own
Half way through some time or other.
When they happen, the mind alerts itself –
It's as if this landscape were suddenly
To become aware
Of the existence of its own elements –
Possessive rock, possessing
Only itself: huge lumbering sea –
That fat-fingered lacemaker who,
By sitting on shells, gives them
Their shapes: mountains
Reaching half way to somewhere or other:
And heather and grass and me
And a gull, as usual
Tuning his bagpipe
And not going on to the tune.

Things there to be noticed.

It takes a sunshaft
To reveal the motes in the air. I wait
For that weather, that sunshaft
To show in the dark room of my mind
That invisible dancing, that
Wayward and ceaseless activity, and I bend

My stone arm up till the hawk
Hovering over the hayfield
Perches fluttering
On my wrist.

To a Pragmatist

You say a splash of water
Means itself, and nothing more.
Well then, what it means to me
Means itself, and nothing less.
The one is as real as the other,
Though I'd no more sit by the fire
With a splash of water
Than you'd wash your face with a meaning.

One day you're going to drown
In a splash of meaning.
It won't be much, but your feet
Won't find the bottom.

Dilemma

I move among sensations
Like a mist moving a landscape about,
Creating a loch where none is, trailing
A slope sideways, turning a two-foot stone
Into a stag, a cliff into a cloud, and being
A befuddled and luminous nowhere
When the sun gets in.
When I am my opaquest self,
What gloom.

If I were completely dispersed,
Which will happen, will happen,
These sensational lochs would be
Green hollows, the stone would suck in its stag,
And cliff, slope and cloud stand
Here, there and there. – But where would I be
To notice them? . . . So I'm afraid
When the sun makes me
Luminous – I thicken myself against him
And move disconsolately
Amongst my gray apparitions
Till I am my opaquest self, and then,
What gloom.

Message Taken

Astonished as if
A stone you held in your hand
Spoke to you, you see for the first time
The capering saint behind
My eyes.
He's always been there,
Exercising himself in a mirthless world
By laughing it
Towards bliss. You didn't suspect him,
Not knowing the arrogant standoffishness
Of saints.

I observe you, too,
Through your astonishment – but
Not for the first time. I've always
Seen that sweet novice, that holy girl,
Bending her brittle glass knees
In a simplicity of adoration that brightens
The cell of your
Most pagan of gestures.

My saint capers and
With the holiest of ha-ha's
Giggles that girl to him – who comes
Astonished as a stone
Would be if it found
It could speak.

Above Inverkirkaig

I watch, across a loch
Where seatrout are leaping,
Suilven and Cul Mor, my
Mountains of mountains,
Looming and pachydermatous in the thin light
Of a clear half moon. Something swells
In my mind, in my self, as though
I were about to be enlarged,
To enclose informations and secrets
That lie just beyond me, that I would utter
In one short, stupendous sentence, to the everlasting
A pregnant feeling that is, naturally, caused
By love.

I know, half-moon struck as I am,
The usual miscarriage will follow. I am beyond
The reach of miracles. And am glad of it,
Thinking that, if this miracle were to happen
This time, it would be as if
Suilven should monstrously
Move over to Cul Mor and after
Coupling through human generations
Drag himself back and sit
By his own lochside, indifferently
Observing on the bogs of Assynt
A litter of tiny Suilvens, each one
The dead spit of his father.

Leader of Men

When he addressed ten thousand
Faces worked by automation
He was filled, exalted afflated
With love and ambition for
His fellowcountrymen – in so far,
Of course,
As they were not incompatible
With the love and ambition he felt
For himself. No sacrifice
Would be too great. No
Holocaust. No bloodbath. He
Was so affected by the nobility
Of his vision, his eyes were,
Naturally, blurred.

How was he to know
The mindless face of the crowd
Broke up, when he finished, into
Ten thousand pieces – except that,
When he went home,
He found the tea cold, his wife
Plain, his dog smelly?

Linguist

If we lived in a world where bells
Truly say "ding-dong" and where "moo"
Is a rather neat thing
Said by a cow,
I could believe you could believe
That these sounds I make in the air
And these shapes with which I blacken
White paper have some reference
To the thoughts in my mind
And the feelings in the thoughts.

As things are,
If I were to gaze in your eyes and say
"Bow-wow" or "quack", you must take that to be
A despairing anthology of praises,
A concentration of all the opposites
Of reticence, a capsule
Of my meaning of meaning
That I can no more write down
Than I could spell the sound of the sigh
I would then utter, before
Dingdonging and mooing my way
Through all the lexicons and languages
Of imprecision.

Monologue in my Head

Crabwise, snailwise, in this little house
I listen to the west wind dashing
Handfuls of miles of rain
On its July roof, and sniff appreciatively
The darling buds
Of May. I lift
A mushroom of snow to my connoisseur's nose
And watch apples rolling
On the cool floor of October. I have a birthday
Every day, ringed in your calendar,
And inhabit – tiny, domestic kraaken –
A gentle maelstrom of seasons. Trout swim
In the appleblossom and the jug of fog
On the windowsill glitters
So much it dances up and down.
Who will explain me to myself,
The sea to the rock, the claw's clasp
To the twig, you
To everything?

I am the green knoll you sing inside
That frightens wayfarers. You are
The processes of my calculation.
How can the air blow by
And go away? How can a stone
Stay still and not follow you?

Questions I know the answers to.
For there you are, a fact
Among facts – no Orpheus
Dislocating landscapes and no
White-faced Euridice being beautiful

Among the shades. The wind goes by
As you will and the stone stays
As you will. And I lounge
In my fireside maelstrom
Of miracles,
Slightly dizzy,
Slightly me,
Fatly remarking the continuous creation
That moves in your moving and multiplies
In your stillness, till being
Overspills and creates
New forms of being
For the surplus.

An Ordinary Day

I took my mind a walk
Or my mind took me a walk –
Whichever was the truth of it.

The light glittered on the water
Or the water glittered in the light.
Cormorants stood on a tidal rock

With their wings spread out,
Stopping no traffic. Various ducks
Shilly-shallied here and there

On the shilly-shallying water.
An occasional gull yelped. Small flowers
Were doing their level best

To bring to their kerb bees like
Aerial charabancs. Long weeds in the clear
Water did Eastern dances, unregarded

By shoals of darning needles. A cow
Started a moo but thought
Better of it . . . And my feet took me home

And my mind observed to me,
Or I to it, how ordinary
Extraordinary things are or

How extraordinary ordinary
Things are, like the nature of the mind
And the process of observing.

A Writer

Events got him in a corner
And gave him a bad time of it –
Poverty, people, ill-health
Battered at him from all sides.
So far from being silenced,
He wrote more poems than ever
And all of them different –
Just as a stoned crow
Invents ways of flying
It had never thought of before.

No wonder now he sometimes
Suddenly lurches, stalls, twirls sideways,
Before continuing his effortless level flight
So high over the heads of people
Their stones can't reach him.

Assisi

The dwarf with his hands on backwards
Sat, slumped like a half-filled sack
On tiny twisted legs from which
Sawdust might run,
Outside the three tiers of churches built
In honour of St. Francis, brother
Of the poor, talker with birds, over whom
He had the advantage
Of not being dead yet.

His look owes its slyness
To the fact
That he had no neck.

A priest explained
How clever it was of Giotto
To make his frescoes tell stories
That would reveal to the illiterate the goodness
Of God and the suffering
Of His Son. I understood
The explanation and
The cleverness.

A rush of tourists, clucking contentedly,
Fluttered after him as he scattered
The grain of the word. It was they who had passed
The ruined temple outside, whose eyes
Wept pus, whose back was higher
Than his head, whose lopsided mouth
Said *Grazie* in a voice as sweet
As a child's when she speaks to her mother
Or a bird's when it spoke
To St. Francis.

Nothing So Memorable

Like an orange pip squeezed from between fingertips
The roebuck shot from the bracken bush
And into the wood. Sudden things
Are apparitions, if they're over
Quickly enough – like a trout
A foot above the water it extravagantly
Emerged from – you remember it
A foot above the water, not coming out
Or returning to it: a still.
Can you tell me
How you manage to be an apparition
All the time?

Or, when I hear that music
Which is my miracle of music, it shows
How much my memory falls short
Of its always new and never changing utterance.
But this requires,
Between my experiences of that music, time
For memory to work in,
And time is that unavoidable process
You disqualify, when
You startle me
To an apprehension of your still self
By an unbroken presence
Of suddennesses:
Stills
Of your stillness.

No Nominalist

I'll say a sunshiny thing
And breed grasshoppers in any
Grass there is, to rollick there,
Playing their green fiddles. Or
I'll say a moonshiny thing and
Fish will curl in the glass wall,
Of any wave going by: you'll smile
At their bright commas. Or I'll say
A rainy thing and snails
Will shine on walls under
Their cocklehats, peaceful pilgrims
Without staffs.

All this so that I won't say
A saying thing, that would uncurtain
A world too real, of
Grasshoppers, fishes, snails and
Me, grinning all round
At such inventions and frightened
To name you in their midst – I'll not
Be Adam and name them, or you,
In case I anger
The friendly archangel and
Learn the meaning
Of the snake's hiss.

Flooded Mind

When the water fell
The trees rose up again
And fish stopped being birds
Among the branches.

The trees were never the same again, though,
And the birds
Often regarded him
With a very fishy eye
As he walked the policies of himself,
His own keeper.

Also, he was afraid to go fishing
In case he landed a fish
With feathers that would sing
In his net.

No wonder his eyes were
Noticeboards saying
Private. Keep out.

Not Stolen, but Strayed

When hog-spawn flounces the castle wall
Might perhaps have been muttered by
Tennyson, morosely drunk, with his ear on
The table and his mind freewheeling
Amongst its bric-à-brac. I am not drunk
Nor Tennyson; but I freewheel, too, and see
His "white owl" hunting
Where Shakespearian
Micicles hang by the wall,
And I realise that, having no game
In my own coverts, I'm poaching
In their preserves with
A scattergun.

The ground you can't see is
The ground you're standing on.
The most invisible landscape is the one
You've stared out of existence.

Let me plant you
In my tiny policies, an exotic tree
That will realise the other ones. Your branches
Will focus them back into being,
And I, perched in them,
Will utter a gingerly
Tu-whoo and tilt my plate of a face
Over the rustling in the undergrowth
Of rats and
Mice and such
Small . . .

. . . Some sorts of silence
Embarrass me. I sing best

Beside a waterfall or a locomotive being
A dragon – but I don't imitate
The waterfall or pretend
To be a dragon. Go away, Tennyson,
Go away every wordmonger and let
My native vocabulary range
Its possibility of meaning, prowling
The familiar and finding there,
Amongst other things, you,
My most native of trees,
My least exotic, splendidly
Making a forest and making a forest
No more than a forest is.

When that happens (as it does)
Metaphors fall away and
My freewheeling mind idles
Through silence, where you
Disqualify appearance by
Including it, in a justice
Of opposites, of silence and words,
Of you there and not there, of
Zero and the first number.

I regard this owlishly
And from your bloomy spray call
Jug-jug tereu in
A most owlish voice,
Still strayed, still hearing
My own words rustling away from me
In my own darkness.

Near Midnight

I hear a bull blaring
From the sad shores of love.

Owls never haunt
The dark rides of this darkness,
So the one now calling over
The hayfield has the voice
Of a prophet returned
From the wilderness.

What wilderness shall I
Go into so that you will listen
When I return?

Under the few stars
Terns are dipping through the air
Towards the green islet
They rest on, quarrel on.
Though they seem half
Reptile, half angel, they
Are closer to me
Than you.
Their silence frightens me
Less than yours. – I listen,
I listen, and hear only
Reeds whispering their language and
A bull – sailor on shore
Calling the sirens in.
And all this
Is wilderness enough
For me.

Hill Streams of Abruzzi

Through Florentine palaces
And the basilicas of Verona
Flow the green streams of Abruzzi.
The canals of Venice slipslop under their water.
And frescoes by great dead men
Waver in an aqueous light that has trickled
Wooingly down
From a desperate landscape
Of wolves and bears.

They have dug channels
In their yellow rocks.
They have dug channels
In the substance of my mind.

They flow by bell-towers
Of ferocious crags.
Between murals of mountains,
Through the harsh mosaics of dead avalanches,
They speak the world language of hill streams.

I listen and understand
That watery Esperanto –
I am
A new valley for them to flow through.

Lesson Time

When Donald speaks sharply to Lassie,
Sandy, her collie-brother, slinks
Out of the house and comes back
Hours later
Stinking of the filth
He has rolled in.

True emblem
Of a pacifist?

When Murphy, the bull, turned on
Lassie, Sandy had two ribs
Staved in before
She got off safely.

True crusader, true
Defender of the weak, true
Patriot?

Don't look for emblems, brother,
Who are yourself a fine
Snapper at heels with useful flocks
On the mountain.

Escapist

Sitting under the wolf's howl,
Watching
A crepitation of violets
Advancing on the shadowy ground,
I play my part
Of the terrified, miraculously preserved
Traveller in dark woods.
How can I dare
Knock at the door of that hovel
Where a woman screams in childbirth?
I turn aside from the axe-shine
And the man smelling of smoke
Who strides ferociously by, re-assembling himself
From a cubism of sun-glints.
The hunting horn twangs, and horses
Crash past the bramble covert
Where I cower, pale and sweating. And
Even the squirrel's claws
Scratch on the delicate membrane
My brain beats under.

Within reach of my hand, the radio
Waits in the silence
I have locked it in. On my walls
Books stand, palms closed together –
I will not accept
What they would offer. I sit
Under the wolf's howl, miraculously
Preserved in the fairytale
I am writing myself, watching
Violets creeping on the shadowy ground
I will never be buried in.

In This Wild Day

You wade through galloping grass
In this parish mythical
With Hebridean cuckoos and corn so alien
It pines for a fatter sunshine, a less
Acid grip to its feet. Your raincoat
Tries to go back home, but your mind,
Hauling on a long purpose, pulls you,
Thought over thought, to
The edge of the sea. There
You stand on a steep rock and throw
Into the galloping water bottles and
Tins – if they won't burn,
They'll drown. They'll rust
To a red web or glitter in the tangle
To the misunderstanding
Of lobsters and congers. – But one
Won't sink and, wearing itself askew,
Drunkenly toddles off towards Harris.

You turn back home, with your coat
For spinnaker and the tide
Of grass in your favour, to where I sit
In my snug ark, the smoke
From its streaming funnel racing
Out of itself over
The slanted cornfield. From it I throw
Used up ideas, empty feelings
To drown in another tide – except this one
That sidles and bobs and makes
Its landfall on this
White shore.

Old Poet

The alder tree
Shrivelled by the salt wind
Has lived so long
It has carried and sheltered
Its own weight
Of nests.

Four O'clock Blackbird

Just when it was possible to think
The darkness was less dark,
I heard a blackbird thoughtfully
Saying what he thought
From a hawthorn tree I'm fond of.
He was slow, but precise. – How lucky
For him not to be restricted, like tits,
To a mechanical rote of notes played
With pianola exactness. And if he didn't have
The acrobatic aplomb of
The wise thrush that says everything twice over,
Like Browning,
He was bronze to the thrush's silver
And, between night and day,
Made a rich sound that said,
Thoughtfully and unhurriedly,
From the heart of a hawthorn tree
I'm more fond of than ever,
That to be between
Night and day is to be
Between two richnesses and
In a third.

Questionnaire

Why, when I praise you, when I tell you
Some not much decorated truth,
Do you look as if a stone, dropped
From your hand, fell
Upward? Are you amazed that I,
Pulpily surrounding my experience of you,
Can see you as you are, decorate
You and believe in both you
And the decoration? Or do you not
Recognise yourself in the truth? or
In the decoration? or in what both
Make of you? Are you amazed that you,
Pulpily surrounded by my experience of you,
Are expanded into it and become
A new truth? And how can I accept
Such amazement from you – I
Who, when you drop a stone,
Look upward?

Loch Roe

Not even the tide
Sighed, being brimful. The moonburnt water
Lay inert and silent as
A deserted city square. Hills rose from it
as steep as tenements. The citizens of the place
Had gone to roost, in cellars
And flats and attics. No trafficking here
Except with silence and stillness.

Enter two policemen, two
Puffing porpoises, that
Patrolled the place, found everything
In order and went off side by side,
Good boys in blue, down the narrow street
They came in by.

It wasn't for some moments after they had gone
That the whole place was again
Under arrest.

Two Shepherds

Donald roared and ran and brandished
His stick and swore
In all the languages
He knew, which were
Some.

Pollóchan sauntered, stood
Six feet three silent: with a small
Turn of the hand
He'd send the collie flowing
Round the mile-long arc
Of a towsy circle.

Two poets –
Dionysian,
Apollonian
And the sheep in the pen.

No Consolation

I consoled myself for not being able to describe
Water trickling down a wall or
A wall being trickled down by water
By reflecting that I can see
These two things are not the same thing:
Which is more than a wall can do,
Or water.
                    – But how hard it is
To live at a remove
From a common wall, that keeps out and
Keeps in, and from water, that
Saves you and drowns you.

But when I went on to notice
That I could see the pair of them
As a trickling wall or as a wall
Of water,
It became clear that I can describe only
My own inventions.
                                    – And how odd to suppose
You prove you love your wife
By continually committing adultery
With her.

Figurations

When we agreed it is possible
To talk about
A geometry of love,
She said it was a circle
Infinitely expansible and all sizes
At the same time, with every other figure
Anchored to its remarkable
Circumference. I said
No, it is a line that starts
From the point ABCD . . . eight down
To Z and shoots straight off
Into space, measuring the shortest distance
To everywhere.
It was only later we realised
We meant the same thing, so we
Contracted that circle and took
The shortest distance
To each other.

Pastoral

Light clouds down, soaking
Through trees, lying heavy
On lumpish water: a gray glaze
On the spouting rock.

No cloud-in-itself wallows
In air that is all cloud, except
For one wisp shredded
By the comb of Stac Polly.

The shot stag runs through
More mists than one,
His lower jaw swinging loose
From burst hinges.

Let him run his fastest,
He will not outstrip
The slow death
That keeps pace with him.

For how many days
Will the light darken before
His empty cage lies, growing green
On the green ground.

Looking Down on Glen Canisp

The summer air is thick, is wads
That muffle the hill burn's voice
And stifle colours to
The colours below them – and
Bright enough: the little loch
Is the one clear pane
In a stained-glass window.

The scent of thyme and bog myrtle
Is so thick one
Listens for it, as though it might be
A drowsy honey-hum
In the heavy air.

Even the ravens
Have sunk into the sandstone cliffs
Of Suilven, that are dazed blue
And fuzz into the air around them –
As my mind does, till I hear
A thin far clatter and
Look down to where two stags
Canter across the ford, splashing up before them
Antlers of water.

Brown Vase

It is as foolish of me
To try to distinguish between
You and your beauty
As to ask, of the brown vase on my bookshelves,
Whether the black lines are there
To decorate the vase
Or whether the vase exists
To make the decoration possible.

Especially as you –
More than it or anything else, more, even,
Than love itself –
Are made of concordances, married
Into one concordance,
As a harmony can be
A plurality of harmonies
Sounding together.

And what a discord I am of pride
And humility and thankfulness
When I think your knowledge of me
Is a new note that has entered
Into that harmony
Without disrupting it.

No Word for It

There's no doubt about it,
"A week" is shorter than "seven days".
Language is a compulsive denier
Of synonyms.

So when I change from being a man who loves you
To being a man who says, "I love you",
I set myself up
As a liar
Who, with practice, will become
A prodigious liar,
Sidling away through one failed synonym after another
From the matter in heart.
I watch it dwindling, I watch it dwindling,
And I don't like it.

Look at it this way:

Seven days are a week
And a week makes seven days shorter,
And therefore a week makes a week shorter.
Where, where will it all end?

Anatomist

I'm tired of your dying
In so many ways at once.

How can I tell which of the pools
You are drowning in
I should plunge into –
Who am no swimmer anyway?

When it's all over, I'll be
Resurrectionist, no doubt –
In a Burke and Hare, not
Christ, way.

How my tears will fall
As my knife slits, my saw
Grates, my hands
Fill with blood.

Absorbed

Each footstep parted
From the sodden earth it clung to
With a vulgar kiss. I breathed webs
And gossamers of water – if you clenched your fist,
I thought, you'd squeeze waterdrops
From mid-air. A hawk flew by,
Almost leaving a wake, and buzzards
Aquaplaned over the ridges.

My mind, snug
In its wren's nest, was its own element,
As it has to be. Yet it could creep into
A tormented thorn bush, a flat palm
Of water, a reed in the wind
Playing an invisible fish. It could wear
The curved nose of an affronted ewe
And tug so, like this, with
A rocking lilypad.

Now at home it spreads out that landscape
Like a chart and follows the course
Pricked on it by a line
Of vulgar kisses. And it knows
That for it this journey will never end.
A transference has been made. A squelching
Countryside has become
A dry thought, and square miles
Fluff their feathers in the wren's nest.

To be one's element
Seems more inhospitable
Than it is.

Walking Home Exhausted

When I lay down by the roadside,
The water being white,
I could believe that
If I fell asleep
I wouldn't wake for seven years.

I didn't want to happen to me
What happened to Thomas the Rhymer –
Especially as he awoke
With a tongue
That could never lie.

What would my friends say?
And how could I bear
The triumphant cries
Of my enemies?